■ Flute

John Kember and Catherine Ramsden

Flute Sight-Reading 1

Déchiffrage pour la flûte 1
Vom-Blatt-Spiel auf der Flöte 1

A fresh approach / Nouvelle approche
Eine erfrischend neue Methode

ED 12817
ISMN M-2201-2378-8

SCHOTT

www.schott-music.com

Mainz · London · Madrid · New York · Paris · Prague · Tokyo · Toronto
© 2006 Schott & Co. Ltd, London · Printed in Germany

Acknowledgments
We would like to thank Margaret Pether, Amy and Chris Lloyd, and Mark Underwood for
their valued support, advice and encouragement during the preparation of this book.

Remerciements
Nous tenons á remercier Margaret Pether, Amy and Chris Lloyd et Mark Underwood de
leur soutien, de leurs conseils et de leurs encouragements inestimables lors de la preparation
de ce recueil.

Danksagung
Wir möchten uns bei Margaret Pether, Amy and Chris Lloyd und Mark Underwood für
ihre wertvolle Unterstützung, ihren Rat und ihre Bestärkung bei der Herstellung dieses
Buches bedanken.

ED 12817

British Library Cataloguing-in-Publication Data.
A catalogue record for this book is available from the British Library
ISMN M-2201-2378-8

© 2006 Schott & Co. Ltd, London

French translation: Agnès Ausseur
German translation: Ute Corleis
Cover design and layout by www.adamhaystudio.com
Music setting and page layout by Jackie Leigh
Printed in Germany S&Co.8040

Contents
Sommaire/Inhalt

Preface

Flute Sight-Reading 1 aims to establish good practice and provide an early introduction to the essential skill of sight-reading.

Sight-reading given as 'homework' is of little value unless the result is heard by the teacher. Ideally, sight-reading in some form should become a regular part of a student's routine each time they play the flute.

This book aims to establish the habit early in a student's flute playing. Of course, names of notes and time values need to be thoroughly known and understood, but equally sight-reading is helped by awareness of shape and direction.

There are eight sections in this book, each of which introduces new notes, rhythms, articulations, dynamics and Italian terms in a logical sequence, much as you would find in a beginner's flute tutor. The emphasis is on providing idiomatic tunes and structures rather than sterile sight-reading exercises. Each section begins with several solo examples and concludes with duets and accompanied pieces, enabling the player to gain experience of sight-reading within the context of ensemble playing.

Section 1 uses the notes B – G, together with simple rhythms and time signatures. Melodic material emphasises movement by step, simple phrase structures, repeated notes and repeated melodic shapes (sequences).

Section 2 introduces the note C, quavers and slurs.

Section 3 introduces F and B♭, and larger jumps of intervals up to a fifth within the melodies. The time signature 5/4 is first encountered here and some of the pieces in this section begin on a beat other than the first beat of the bar.

Section 4 extends to D, includes F♯ and introduces accidentals and dotted crotchets. Greater challenges are presented in the rhythms and counting of rests.

Section 5 has further examples of dotted rhythms, extends to a range from low E to high A, and the key of E minor is introduced.

Section 6 sets up compound time using 3/8, 6/8 and 9/8. Semiquavers are first encountered here and the section explores new keys, including the key of C minor.

Section 7 presents more on compound time and extends the range from low E♭ to high B.

Section 8 concludes book 1 and brings together all the elements so far encountered: simple and compound time signatures, key signatures up to three sharps or three flats, various articulations, rhythmic elements, rests, and ensemble sight-reading, all within a range of two octaves from low to high D.

To the pupil: why sight-reading?

When you are faced with a new piece and asked to play it, whether at home, in a lesson or in an exam or audition, there is no one there to help you – except yourself! Sight-reading tests your ability to read the time and notes correctly and to observe the phrasing and dynamics quickly.

The aim of this book is to help you to teach yourself. The book gives guidance on what to look for and how best to prepare in a very short time by observing the time and key signatures, the shape of the melody and the marks of expression. These short pieces progress gradually to help you to build up your confidence and observation, and enable you to sight-read accurately. At the end of each section there are duets to play with your teacher or friends and pieces with piano accompaniment, which will test your ability to sight-read while something else is going on. This is a necessary skill when playing with a band, orchestra or other ensemble.

If you sight-read something every time you play your flute you will be amazed how much better you will become. Remember, if you can sight-read most of the tunes you are asked to learn you will be able to concentrate on the 'tricky bits' and complete them quickly.

Think of the tunes in this book as 'mini-pieces' and try to learn them quickly and correctly. Then when you are faced with real sight-reading you will be well equipped to succeed on a first attempt.

You are on your own now!

Préface

Le propos de ce recueil de déchiffrage pour la flûte est de fournir une première initiation et un entraînement solide aux principes de la lecture à vue.

Le déchiffrage imposé comme un « travail » ne présente pas grand intérêt s'il n'est supervisé par le maître. L'idéal serait que le déchiffrage prenne régulièrement place dans la routine de travail de l'élève à chaque fois qu'il prend sa flûte.

L'objectif est ici d'établir l'habitude de la lecture à vue très tôt dans l'étude de la flûte. Le déchiffrage suppose, bien sûr, que les noms et les valeurs de notes soient complètement assimilés et compris mais il s'appuie également sur la reconnaissance des contours et de la direction.

Ce volume comporte huit sections correspondant à l'introduction progressive de notes, de rythmes, de phrasés, de nuances et de termes italiens nouveaux selon la progression logique rencontrée dans un méthode de flûte pour débutant. La démarche consiste à fournir des airs et des structures idiomatiques propres à la flûte de préférence à de stériles exercices de déchiffrage. Chaque section débute par plusieurs exemples de solos et se termine par des duos et des morceaux accompagnés destinés à familiariser avec le déchiffrage lors de l'exécution collective.

La section 1 se concentre sur les notes *si* à *sol* associées à des rythmes et des indications de mesures simples. Le mouvement mélodique insiste sur la progression par degrés, les structures de phrases simples, les notes répétées et la répétition de motifs mélodiques (séquences).

La section 2 introduit la note *do*, les croches et les liaisons.

La section 3 introduit les notes *fa* et *si*♭ et les sauts d'intervalles jusqu'à la quinte à l'intérieur des mélodies. L'indication de mesure 5/4 apparaît ici pour la première fois et certaines pièces de cette section commencent sur un autre temps que le premier temps de la mesure.

La section 4 s'étend jusqu'au *ré*, comprend le *fa*♯ et introduit des altérations accidentelles et des noires pointées. Les rythmes et la battue des silences exigent une plus grande attention.

La section 5 présente d'autres rythmes pointés, une tessiture étendue du *mi* grave au *la* aigu et l'introduction de la tonalité de *mi* mineur.

La section 6 se tourne vers les mesures composées à 3/8, 6/8 et 9/8. Les doubles croches y apparaissent pour la première fois et de nouvelles tonalités y sont abordées dont celle de *do* mineur.

La section 7 approfondit l'approche des mesures composées et élargit la tessiture du *mi*♭ grave au *si* aigu.

La section 8 conclut le volume 1 et rassemble tous les éléments rencontrés précédemment : mesures simples et composées, tonalités comportant jusqu'à trois dièses ou trois bémols, phrasés divers, éléments rythmiques, silences et déchiffrage collectif dans une tessiture s'étendant sur deux octaves du *ré* grave au *ré* aigu.

A l'élève : Pourquoi le déchiffrage ?

Lorsque vous vous trouvez face à un nouveau morceau que l'on vous demande de jouer, que ce soit chez vous, pendant une leçon, pour accompagner un autre instrumentiste ou lors d'un examen ou d'une audition, personne d'autre ne peut vous aider que vous-même ! Le déchiffrage met à l'épreuve votre capacité à lire correctement les rythmes et les notes et à observer rapidement le phrasé et les nuances.

Ce recueil se propose de vous aider à vous entraîner vous-même. Il vous oriente sur ce que vous devez repérer et sur la meilleure manière de vous préparer en un laps de temps très court en sachant observer les indications de mesure et l'armure de la clef, les contours de la mélodie et les indications expressives. Ces pièces brèves, en progressant par étapes, vous feront prendre de l'assurance, aiguiseront vos observations et vous permettront de lire à vue avec exactitude et aisance. A la fin de chaque section figurent des duos que vous pourrez jouer avec votre professeur ou des amis et des morceaux avec accompagnement de piano qui vous apprendront à déchiffrer pendant que se déroule une autre partie. Cette capacité est indispensable pour jouer dans un groupe, un orchestre ou un ensemble.

Vous serez stupéfait de vos progrès si vous déchiffrez une pièce à chaque fois que vous vous mettez à la flûte. N'oubliez pas que si vous êtes capable de lire à vue la plupart des morceaux que vous allez étudier, vous pourrez vous concentrer sur les passages difficiles et les assimiler plus vite.

Considérez ces pages comme des « mini-morceaux » et essayez de les apprendre rapidement et sans erreur de manière à ce que, devant un véritable déchiffrage, vous soyez bien armé pour réussir dès la première lecture.

Vous êtes désormais seul !

Vorwort

Vom-Blatt-Spiel auf der Flöte 1 möchte zu einer guten Übetechnik verhelfen und frühzeitig für die Einführung der grundlegenden Fähigkeit des Blatt-Spiels sorgen.

Vom-Blatt-Spiel als Hausaufgabe aufzugeben hat wenig Sinn, wenn das Ergebnis nicht vom Lehrer überprüft wird. Idealerweise sollte das Vom-Blatt-Spiel in irgendeiner Form ein regelmäßiger Bestandteil des Übens werden.

Dieses Buch hat zum Ziel, bereits von Anfang an diese Gewohnheit in das Flötenspiel des Schülers zu verankern. Natürlich muss man die Notennamen und Notenwerte komplett kennen und verstanden haben, aber durch das Bewusstsein für Form und Richtung wird das Vom-Blatt-Spiel gleichermaßen unterstützt.

Das Buch hat acht Teile, die nach und nach neue Noten, Rhythmen, Artikulation, Dynamik und italienische Begriffe in einer logischen Abfolge einführen - ganz ähnlich, wie man es in einer Flötenschule für Anfänger auch finden würde. Der Schwerpunkt liegt auf dem Bereitstellen passender Melodien und Strukturen anstelle von sterilen Vom-Blatt-Spiel Übungen. Jeder Teil beginnt mit einigen Solobeispielen und endet mit Duetten und begleiteten Stücken, damit man auch beim Zusammenspiel mit anderen Erfahrungen mit dem Blattspiel sammeln kann.

Teil 1 benutzt die Töne g^1 – h^1 zusammen mit einfachen Rhythmen und Taktarten. Das melodische Material beschäftigt sich mit schrittweiser Bewegung, einfach strukturierten Phrasen sowie sich wiederholenden Noten und melodischen Formen (Sequenzen).

Teil 2 führt den Ton c^2, Achtelnoten und Bindungen ein.

Teil 3 führt die Töne f^1 und b^1 ein. Innerhalb der Melodien gibt es größere Intervallsprünge bis hin zur Quinte. Die Taktart 5/4 wird zum ersten Mal vorgestellt und einige Stücke dieses Teiles beginnen mit einem Auftakt.

Teil 4 erweitert den Tonraum um das d^2 und das fis^1 und führt sowohl Notenvorzeichen als auch punktierte Viertelnoten ein. Außerdem werden die Anforderungen in Bezug auf die Rhythmen und das Zählen von Pausen größer.

Teil 5 beinhaltet weitere Beispiele für punktierte Rhythmen und erweitert den Tonraum vom e^1 bis zum a^2. Darüber hinaus wird die Tonart e-Moll eingeführt.

Teil 6 beschäftigt sich mit den zusammengesetzten Taktarten 3/8, 6/8 und 9/8. Es kommen zum ersten Mal Sechzehntelnoten vor sowie neue Tonarten – darunter auch c-Moll.

In Teil 7 gibt es noch mehr zusammengesetzte Taktarten und einen Notenumfang von es^1 bis h^2.

Teil 8 beendet Buch 1. Darin werden alle bisher eingeführten Elemente zusammengebracht: einfache und zusammengesetzte Taktarten, Tonarten bis zu drei Kreuzen und drei Bs, unterschiedliche Artikulationsarten, rhythmische Elemente, Pausen und Vom-Blatt-Spiel mit anderen. Alles findet in einem Tonraum von zwei Oktaven statt, von d^1 bis h^2.

An den Schüler: Warum Vom-Blatt-Spiel?

Wenn du dich einem neuen Musikstück gegenüber siehst und gebeten wirst, es zu spielen, egal, ob zu Hause, im Unterricht, in einem Examen oder einem Vorspiel, gibt es niemanden, der dir helfen kann – nur du selbst! Das Blatt-Spiel testet die Fähigkeit, die Taktart und die Noten richtig zu lesen sowie Phrasierungen und Dynamik schnell zu erfassen.

Ziel dieses Buches ist es, dir beim Selbstunterricht behilflich zu sein. Das Buch zeigt dir, worauf du achten sollst und wie du dich in sehr kurzer Zeit am besten vorbereitest. Das tust du, indem du dir Takt- und Tonart genau anschaust. Die kurzen Musikstücke steigern sich nur allmählich, um sowohl dein Vertrauen und deine Beobachtungsgabe aufzubauen als auch, um dich dazu zu befähigen, exakt vom Blatt zu spielen. Am Ende jeden Teils stehen Duette, die du mit deinem Lehrer oder deinen Freunden spielen kannst. Außerdem gibt es Stücke mit Klavierbegleitung, die deine Fähigkeit im Blatt-Spiel überprüfen, während gleichzeitig etwas anderes abläuft. Das ist eine wesentliche Fähigkeit, wenn man mit einer Band, einem Orchester oder einer anderen Musikgruppe zusammenspielt.

Wenn du jedes Mal, wenn du Flöte spielst, auch etwas vom Blatt spielst, wirst du überrascht sein, wie sehr du dich verbesserst. Denke daran: wenn du die meisten Melodien, die du spielen sollst, vom Blatt spielen kannst, kannst du dich auf die ‚schwierigen Teile' konzentrieren und diese viel schneller beherrschen.

Stelle dir die Melodien in diesem Buch als ‚Ministücke' vor und versuche, sie schnell und korrekt zu lernen. Wenn du dann wirklich vom Blatt spielen musst, wirst du bestens ausgerüstet sein, um gleich beim ersten Versuch erfolgreich zu sein.

Jetzt bist du auf dich selbst gestellt!

Section 1 – Notes G, A and B
Section 1 – Notes *sol*, *la* et *si*
Teil 1 – Die Töne g^1, a^1 und h^1

Three steps to success

1. **Look at the top number of the time signature**. It shows the number of beats in a bar. Tap (clap, sing or play on one note) the rhythm, feeling the pulse throughout. Count at least one bar of the time signature in your head to set up the pulse before you tap or play each tune.

2. **Look for patterns**. While tapping the rhythm, look at the melodic shape and notice movement by step, skips, repeated notes and sequences (a short, repeated melodic phrase which often rises or falls by step).

3. **Keep going**. Remember: a wrong note or rhythm can be corrected the next time you play it. If you stop, you have doubled the mistake!

Trois étapes vers la réussite

1. **Observez le chiffre supérieur de l'indication de mesure**. Il indique le nombre de pulsations contenues par mesure. Frappez (dans les mains, chantez ou jouez sur une seule note) le rythme tout en maintenant une pulsation intérieure constante. Comptez mentalement au moins une mesure complète pour installer la pulsation avant de frapper ou de jouer chaque pièce.

2. **Repérez les motifs**. Tout en frappant le rythme, observez les contours de la mélodie et relevez les mouvements par degrés, les sauts d'intervalles, les notes répétées et les séquences (courtes phrases mélodiques répétées progressant généralement par degrés ascendants ou descendants).

3. **Ne vous arrêtez pas**. Vous corrigerez une fausse note ou rythme inexact la prochaine fois que vous jouerez. Si vous vous interrompez, vous doublez la faute !

Drei Schritte zum Erfolg

1. **Schaue dir die obere Zahl der Taktangabe an**. Diese zeigt die Anzahl der Schläge in einem Takt. Schlage (klatsche, singe oder spiele auf einer Note) den Rhythmus, wobei du immer das Metrum spürst. Zähle mindestens einen Takt lang die Taktangabe im Kopf, um das Metrum zu verinnerlichen, bevor du jede der Melodien klopfst oder spielst.

2. **Achte auf Muster**. Schaue dir die melodische Form an, während du den Rhythmus schlägst und achte auf Bewegungen in Schritten oder Sprüngen, sich wiederholende Noten und Sequenzen (eine kurze, sich wiederholende melodische Phrase, die oft schrittweise ansteigt oder abfällt).

3. **Bleibe dran**. Denke daran: eine falsche Note oder ein falscher Rhythmus kann beim nächsten Mal korrigiert werden. Wenn du aber aufhörst zu spielen, verdoppelst du den Fehler!

Section 1 – Notes G, A and B
Section 1 – Notes *sol, la* et *si*
Teil 1 – Die Töne g¹, a¹ und h¹

Play at a steady speed and with a bold tone. Notice the melodic shapes.

Jouer à vitesse régulière et avec une sonorité ferme. Observez les contours mélodiques.

Spiele in einem gleichmäßigen Tempo mit einem kräftigen Ton. Achte auf die melodischen Figuren.

1.

2.

3.

4.

5.

6.

7.

8.

9.

10.

11.

12.

9

13.

14.

15.

16.

17.

18.

19.

20.

Section 2 – Notes G to C; slurs and quavers
Section 2 – Notes *sol* à *do* ; liaisons et croches
Teil 2 – Die Töne g^1 bis c^2; Bindungen und Achtel

Four steps to success

1. **Look at the top number of the time signature.** Tap (clap, sing or play on one note) the rhythm, feeling the pulse throughout. Count at least one bar of the time signature in your head to set up the pulse before you tap or play the tune.

2. **Look for patterns.** While tapping the rhythm, look at the melodic shape and notice movement by step, skips, repeated notes or sequences.

3. **Notice the slurring.** Often, slurring is very logical. Similar phrases will usually have the same articulation.

4. **Keep going!**

Quatre étapes vers la réussite

1. **Observez le chiffre supérieur de l'indication de mesure**. Il indique le nombre de pulsations contenues par mesure. Frappez (dans les mains, chantez ou jouez sur une seule note) le rythme tout en maintenant une pulsation intérieure constante. Comptez mentalement au moins une mesure pour installer la pulsation avant de frappez ou de jouer chaque pièce.

2. **Repérez les motifs**. Tout en frappant le rythme, observez les contours de la mélodie et relevez les mouvements par degrés, les sauts d'intervalles, les notes répétées ou les séquences.

3. **Observez les liaisons de phrasé**. Les liaisons suivent généralement une logique. Les phrases similaires sont habituellement articulées de la même façon.

4. **Ne vous arrêtez pas !**

Vier Schritte zum Erfolg

1. **Schaue dir die obere Zahl der Taktangabe an**. Diese zeigt die Anzahl der Schläge in einem Takt. Schlage (klatsche, singe oder spiele auf einer Note) den Rhythmus, wobei du immer das Metrum spürst. Zähle mindestens einen Takt lang die Taktangabe im Kopf, um das Metrum zu verinnerlichen, bevor du jede der Melodien klopfst oder spielst.

2. **Achte auf Muster**. Schaue dir die melodische Form an, während du den Rhythmus schlägst und achte auf Bewegungen in Schritten oder Sprüngen, sich wiederholende Noten und Sequenzen.

3. **Konzentriere dich auf die Bindungen**. Bindungen sind oft sehr logisch. Ähnliche Phrasen haben normalerweise auch dieselbe Artikulation.

4. **Bleibe dran!**

Section 2 – Notes G to C; slurs and quavers

Section 2 – Notes *sol* à *do* ; liaisons et croches

Teil 2 – Die Töne g[1] bis c[2]; Bindungen und Achtel

Introducing slurs and quavers.

Introduction des liaisons de phrasé et des croches.

Einführung von Bindungen und Achteln.

Notice the slurs.

Observez les liaisons de phrasé.

Achte auf die Bindungen.

14

Look for the pairs of quavers. Repérez les croches par paires. Halte nach Achtelpaaren ♫ Ausschau.

25.

26.

27.

28.

29.

30.

31.

32.

33.

34.

35.

36.

37.

38.

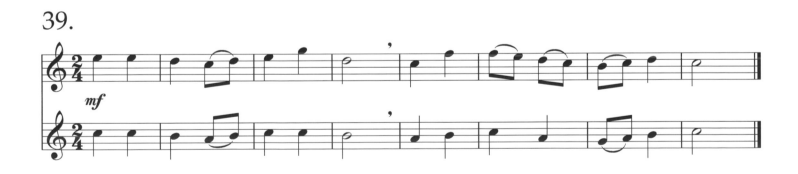

39.

40.

41.

42.

Section 3 – Introducing F and B♭
Section 3 – Introduction de *fa* et *si*♭
Teil 3 – Einführung der Töne f¹ und b¹

Five steps to success

1. **Look at the top number of the time signature**. It shows the number of beats in a bar. Tap (or clap, sing or play on one note) the rhythm, feeling the pulse throughout. Count at least one bar of the time signature in your head to set up the pulse before you tap or play each tune.

2. **Look between the treble clef and the time signature for any sharps or flats.** This is known as the key signature. Make sure you know which notes these apply to and notice where they occur in the melody.

3. **Look for patterns**. While tapping the rhythm, look at the melodic shape and notice movement by step, skips, repeated notes and sequences (a short, repeated melodic phrase which often rises or falls by step).

4. **Notice the articulation and dynamics**. Observe the dynamic shapes and notice if they change suddenly or gradually.

5. **Keep going!**

Cinq étapes vers la réussite

1. **Observez le chiffre supérieur de l'indication de mesure**. Il indique le nombre de pulsations contenues par mesure. Frappez (dans les mains, chantez ou jouez sur un seule note) le rythme tout en maintenant une pulsation intérieure constante. Comptez mentalement au moins une mesure pour installer la pulsation avant de frapper ou de jouer chaque pièce.

2. **Vérifiez les dièses ou les bémols placés entre la clef de *sol* et les chiffres indicateurs de mesure**. Ceux-ci constituent l'armure de la tonalité. Assurez-vous des notes altérées et repérez-les dans la mélodie.

3. **Repérez les motifs**. Tout en frappant le rythme, observez les contours de la mélodie et relevez les déplacements par degrés, les sauts d'intervalles, les notes répétées et les séquences (courte phrase mélodique répétées progressant généralement par degrés ascendants ou descendants).

4. **Observez le phrasé et les nuances**. Notez les nuances dynamiques et leurs changements subits ou progressifs.

5. **Ne vous arrêtez pas !**

Fünf Schritte zum Erfolg

1. **Schaue dir die obere Zahl der Taktangabe an**. Diese zeigt die Anzahl der Schläge in einem Takt. Schlage (klatsche, singe oder spiele auf einer Note) den Rhythmus, wobei du immer das Metrum spürst. Zähle mindestens einen Takt lang die Taktangabe im Kopf, um das Metrum zu verinnerlichen, bevor du jede der Melodien klopfst oder spielst.

2. **Achte auf Kreuz- und B-Vorzeichen zwischen dem Notenschlüssel und der Taktangabe**. Überzeuge dich davon, dass du weißt, auf welche Noten sich diese beziehen und finde heraus, wo in der Melodie sie auftauchen.

3. **Achte auf Muster**. Schaue dir die melodische Form an, während du den Rhythmus schlägst und achte auf Bewegungen in Schritten oder Sprüngen, sich wiederholende Noten und Sequenzen (eine kurze, sich wiederholende melodische Phrase, die oft schrittweise ansteigt oder abfällt).

4. **Beachte Artikulation und Dynamik**. Schaue dir die dynamischen Formen genau an und registriere, ob sie sich plötzlich oder allmählich ändern.

5. **Bleibe dran!**

Performance directions used in this section:

A tempo	at the original tempo
Adagio	slowly
Allegretto	moderately fast
Andante	at a walking pace
Andantino	a little faster than Andante
Con grazia	gracefully
Con moto	with movement
Crescendo (*cresc.*)	getting louder
Dolce	sweetly
Espressivo	expressively
Giocoso	joyfully
Legato	smoothly
Maestoso	majestically
Marcato	marked
Moderato	at a moderate speed
Poco a poco	little by little
Risoluto	resolute
Rallentando (rall.)	becoming gradually slower
Ritardando (rit.)	getting slower
Sostenuto	sustained

Indications d'exécution utilisées dans cette section :

A tempo
Adagio
Allegretto
Andante
Andantino
Con grazia
Con moto
Crescendo (*cresc.*)

Dolce
Espressivo
Giocoso
Legato
Maestoso
Marcato
Moderato
Poco a poco
Risoluto
Rallentando (rall.)

Ritardando (rit.)

Sostenuto

Vortragsangaben, die in diesem Teil verwendet werden:

A tempo	im Grundtempo
Adagio	langsam
Allegretto	gemäßigt schnell
Andante	gehend
Andantino	ein bisschen schneller als Andante
Con grazia	mit Anmut
Con moto	mit Bewegung
Crescendo (*cresc.*)	lauter werdend
Dolce	süß
Espressivo	ausdrucksvoll
Giocoso	scherzhaft
Legato	gebunden
Maestoso	majestätisch
Marcato	markiert
Moderato	gemäßigt
Poco a poco	nach un nach
Risoluto	entschieden
Rallentando (rall.)	allmählich langsamer werdend
Ritardando (rit.)	langsamer werdend
Sostenuto	zurückhaltend

Section 3 – Introducing F and B♭
Section 3 – Introduction de *fa* et *si*♭
Teil 3 – Einführung der Töne f¹ und b¹

43.

This piece begins on the fourth beat of the bar in 4-time.	Cette pièce débute sur le 4e temps d'une mesure à 4 temps.	Dieses Stück beginnt auf dem vierten Schlag in einem 4/4-Takt.
Count 1 2 3 before you begin.	Comptez 1, 2, 3, avant de commencer.	Zähle 1 2 3 vor, bevor du anfängst.

44.

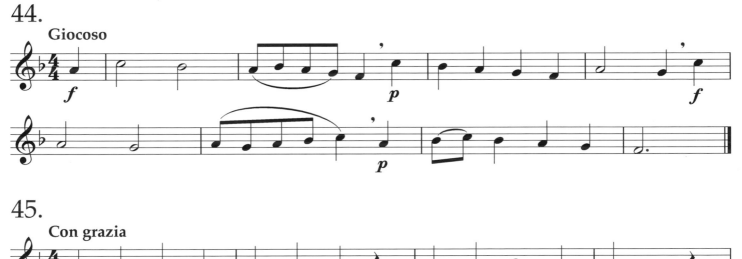

45.

46.

47.

48.

Maestoso

49.

Andante

50.

Adagio

51.

Allegretto

52.

Legato

53.

Andantino

This piece begins on the third beat of the bar in 3-time.
Count 1 2 3 1 2 before you begin.

Cette pièce débute sur le 3e temps d'une mesure à 3 temps.
Comptez 1, 2, 3, 1, 2, avant de commencer.

Dieses Stück beginnt auf dem dritten Schlag in einem 3/4-Takt.
Zähle 1 2 3 1 2 vor, bevor du anfängst.

54.

Risoluto

This piece is in 5-time.
Count 1 2 3 4 5.

Cette pièce est à 5 temps.
Comptez 1, 2, 3, 4, 5.

Dieses Stück ist in einem 5/4-Takt.
Zähle 1 2 3 4 5 vor.

This piece begins on the third beat of the bar in 3-time.
Count 1 2 3 1 2 before you begin.

Cette pièce débute sur le 3e temps d'une mesure à 3 temps.
Comptez 1, 2, 3, 1, 2, avant de commencer.

Dieses Stück beginnt auf dem dritten Schlag in einem 3/4-Takt.
Zähle 1 2 3 1 2 vor, bevor du anfängst.

This piece begins on the fourth beat of the bar in 4-time.
Count 1 2 3 before you begin.

Cette pièce débute sur le 4e temps d'une mesure à 4 temps.
Comptez 1, 2, 3, avant de commencer.

Dieses Stück beginnt auf dem vierten Schlag in einem 4/4-Takt.
Zähle 1 2 3 vor, bevor du anfängst.

60.

Maestoso

61.

Con grazia

62.

Canon

63.

Allegretto

23

64.

65.

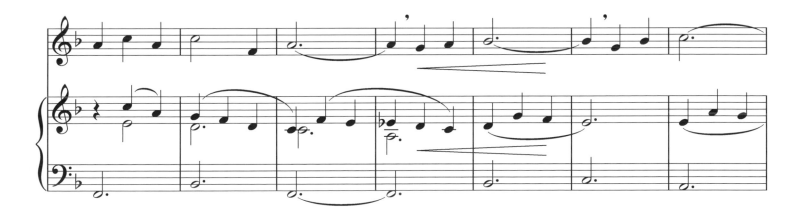

66.

67.

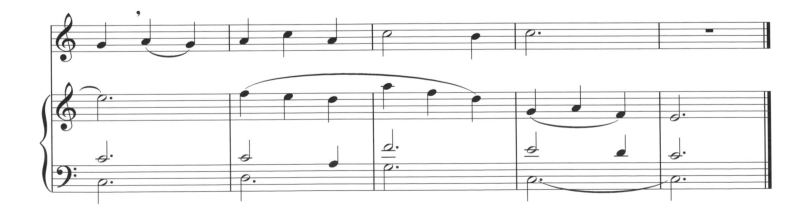

Section 4 – Notes F to D, with F♯ and B♭
Section 4 – Notes *fa* à *ré*, avec *fa*♯ et *si*♭
Teil 4 – Die Töne *f*1 bis *d*2, mit *fis*1 und *b*1

Five steps to success

1. **Look at the top number of the time signature**. It shows the number of beats in a bar. Tap (clap, sing or play on one note) the rhythm, feeling the pulse throughout. Count at least one bar of the time signature in your head to set up the pulse before you tap or play each tune.

2. **Look between the treble clef and the time signature for any sharps and flats**. This is known as the key signature. Make sure you know which notes these apply to and notice where they occur in the melody.

3. **Look for patterns**. While tapping the rhythms, look at the melodic shape and notice movement by step, skips, repeated notes and sequences (a short, repeated melodic phrase which often rises or falls by step).

4. **Notice the articulation and dynamics**. Observe the dynamic shapes and notice if they change suddenly or gradually.

5. **Keep going!**

Performance directions used in this section:

Andante	at walking pace
Andantino	a little faster than Andante
Alla marcia	in a marching style
Cantabile	in a singing style
Con grazia	with grace
Con moto	with movement
Dolce	sweetly
Giocoso	joyfully
Marcato	marked
Maestoso	majestically
Moderato	at a moderate pace
Risoluto	resolutely
Sostenuto	sustained
Vivace	lively

Cinq étapes vers la réussite

1. **Observez le chiffre supérieur de l'indication de mesure**. Il indique le nombre de pulsations contenues par mesure. Frappez (dans les mains, chantez ou jouez sur un seule note) le rythme tout en maintenant une pulsation intérieure constante. Comptez mentalement au moins une mesure pour installer la pulsation avant de frapper ou de jouer chaque pièce.

2. **Vérifiez les dièses ou les bémols placés entre la clef de *sol* et les chiffres indicateurs de mesure**. Ceux-ci constituent l'armure de la tonalité. Assurez-vous des notes altérées et repérez-les dans la mélodie.

3. **Repérez les motifs**. Tout en frappant le rythme, observez les contours de la mélodie et relevez les déplacements par degrés, les sauts d'intervalles, les notes répétées et les séquences (courte phrase mélodique répétées progressant généralement par degrés ascendants ou descendants).

4. **Observez le phrasé et les nuances**. Notez les nuances dynamiques et leurs changements subits ou progressifs.

5. **Ne vous arrêtez pas !**

Indications d'exécution utilisées dans cette section :

Andante	allant
Andantino	un peu plus vite qu'Andante
Alla marcia	comme une marche
Cantabile	chantant
Con grazia	avec grâce
Dolce	doux
Giocoso	joyeux
Marcato	marqué
Maestoso	majestueux
Moderato	modéré
Risoluto	résolu
Sostenuto	soutenu
Vivace	vivement

Fünf Schritte zum Erfolg

1. **Schaue dir die obere Zahl der Taktangabe an**. Diese zeigt die Anzahl der Schläge in einem Takt. Schlage (klatsche, singe oder spiele auf einer Note) den Rhythmus, wobei du immer das Metrum spürst. Zähle mindestens einen Takt lang die Taktangabe im Kopf, um das Metrum zu verinnerlichen, bevor du jede der Melodien klopfst oder spielst.

2. **Achte auf Kreuz- und B-Vorzeichen zwischen dem Notenschlüssel und der Taktangabe**. Versichere dich, dass du weißt, auf welche Noten sich diese beziehen und finde heraus, wo in der Melodie sie auftauchen.

3. **Achte auf Muster**. Schaue dir die melodische Form an, während du den Rhythmus schlägst und achte auf Bewegungen in Schritten oder Sprüngen, sich wiederholende Noten und Sequenzen (eine kurze, sich wiederholende melodische Phrase, die oft schrittweise ansteigt oder abfällt).

4. **Beachte Artikulation und Dynamik**. Schaue dir die dynamischen Formen genau an und registriere, ob sie sich plötzlich oder allmählich ändern.

5. **Bleibe dran!**

Vortragsangaben, die in diesem Teil verwendet werden:

Andante	gehend
Andantino	ein bisschen schneller als Andante
Alla marcia	marschmäßig
Cantabile	gesangvoll
Con grazia	mit Anmut
Con moto	mit Bewegung
Dolce	süß
Giocoso	scherzhaft
Marcato	markiert
Maestoso	majestätisch
Moderato	gemäßigt
Risoluto	entschieden
Sostenuto	zurückhaltend
Vivace	lebhaft

Section 4 – Notes F to D, with F♯ and B♭

Section 4 – Notes *fa* à *ré*, avec *fa*♯ et *si*♭
Teil 4 – Die Töne *f*¹ bis *d*², mit *fis*¹ und *b*¹

68.

This piece begins on the third beat of the bar in 3-time.
Count 1 2 3 1 2 before you begin.

Cette pièce débute sur le 3e temps d'une mesure à 3 temps.
Comptez 1, 2, 3, 1, 2, avant de commencer.

Dieses Stück beginnt auf dem dritten Schlag in einem 3/4-Takt.
Zähle 1 2 3 1 2 vor, bevor du anfängst.

This piece begins on the fourth beat of the bar in 4-time.
Count 1 2 3 before you begin.

Cette pièce débute sur le 4e temps d'une mesure à 4 temps.
Comptez 1, 2, 3, avant de commencer.

Dieses Stück beginnt auf dem vierten Schlag in einem 4/4-Takt.
Zähle 1 2 3 vor, bevor du anfängst.

73. Alla marcia

74. Giocoso

This piece begins on the fourth beat of the bar in 4-time. Count 1 2 3 before you begin.

Cette pièce débute sur le 4e temps d'une mesure à 4 temps. Comptez 1, 2, 3, avant de commencer.

Dieses Stück beginnt auf dem vierten Schlag in einem 4/4-Takt. Zähle 1 2 3 vor, bevor du anfängst.

75. Con moto

Look out for B♭ and B♮.

Recherchez les *si* ♭ et les *si* ♮.

Achte auf die Töne b und h.

76. Marcato

Introducing ♩. ♪ in 3-time.   Introduction du rythme ♩. ♪ dans la mesure à 3 temps.   Einführung von ♩. ♪ im 3/4-Takt.

77.

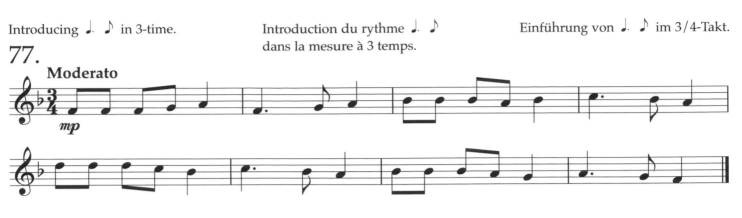

Introducing ♩. ♪ in 4-time.   Introduction du rythme ♩. ♪ dans la mesure à 4 temps.   Einführung von ♩. ♪ im 4/4-Takt.

78.

79.

80.

81.

This piece begins on the third beat
of the bar in 3-time.
Count 1 2 3 1 2 before you begin.

Cette pièce débute sur le 3e temps
d'une mesure à 3 temps.
Comptez 1, 2, 3, 1, 2, avant de
commencer.

Dieses Stück beginnt auf dem
dritten Schlag in einem 3/4-Takt.
Zähle 1 2 3 1 2 vor, bevor du
anfängst.

86.

Andantino

87.

Cantabile

88.

Vivace

89.

90.

91.

92.

93.

94.

Section 5 – Extending the range to top A
Section 5 – Extension de la tessiture jusqu'au *la* aigu
Teil 5 – Ausdehnung des Tonraums bis zum a²

Five steps to success

1. **Look at the top number of the time signature**. It shows the number of beats in a bar. Tap (clap, sing or play on one note) the rhythm, feeling the pulse throughout. Count at least one bar of the time signature in your head to set up the pulse before you tap or play each tune.

2. **Look between the treble clef and the time signature for any sharps or flats**. This is known as the key signature. Make sure you know which notes these apply to and notice where they occur in the melody.

3. **Look for patterns**. While tapping the rhythm, look at the melodic shape and notice movement by step, skips, repeated notes and sequences (a short, repeated melodic phrase which often rises or falls by step).

4. **Notice the articulation and dynamics**. Observe the dynamic shapes and notice if they change suddenly or gradually.

5. **Keep going!**

Performance directions used in this section:

Allegretto	rather lively, though not as much as allegro
Animato	animated
Cantabile	in a singing style
Con brio	with vigour
Con moto	with movement
Dolce	sweetly
Espressivo	expressively
Grazioso	gracefully
Legato	smoothly
Lento	slowly
Lilting	a gently swinging rhythm
Maestoso	majestically
Moderato	moderate time
Vivace	quick / lively

Cinq étapes vers la réussite

1. **Observez le chiffre supérieur de l'indication de mesure**. Il indique le nombre de pulsations contenues par mesure. Frappez (dans les mains, chantez ou jouez sur un seule note) le rythme tout en maintenant une pulsation intérieure constante. Comptez mentalement au moins une mesure pour installer la pulsation avant de frapper ou de jouer chaque pièce.

2. **Vérifiez les dièses ou les bémols placés entre la clef de *sol* et les chiffres indicateurs de mesure**. Ceux-ci constituent l'armure de la tonalité. Assurez-vous des notes altérées et repérez-les dans la mélodie.

3. **Repérez les motifs**. Tout en frappant le rythme, observez les contours de la mélodie et relevez les déplacements par degrés, les sauts d'intervalles, les notes répétées et les séquences (courte phrase mélodique répétées progressant généralement par degrés ascendants ou descendants).

4. **Observez le phrasé et les nuances**. Notez les nuances dynamiques et leurs changements subits ou progressifs.

5. **Ne vous arrêtez pas !**

Indications d'exécution utilisées dans cette section :

Allegretto	assez rapide (moins qu'Allegro)
Animato	animé
Cantabile	chantant
Con brio	avec éclat
Con moto	avec mouvement
Dolce	doux
Espressivo	expressif
Grazioso	gracieux
Legato	lié
Lento	lent
Lilting	rythme balancé
Maestoso	majestueux
Moderato	modéré
Vivace	vivement

Fünf Schritte zum Erfolg

1. **Schaue dir die obere Zahl der Taktangabe an**. Diese zeigt die Anzahl der Schläge in einem Takt. Schlage (klatsche, singe oder spiele auf einer Note) den Rhythmus, wobei du immer das Metrum spürst. Zähle mindestens einen Takt lang die Taktangabe im Kopf, um das Metrum zu verinnerlichen, bevor du jede der Melodien klopfst oder spielst.

2. **Achte auf Kreuz- und B-Vorzeichen zwischen dem Notenschlüssel und der Taktangabe**. Versichere dich, dass du weißt, auf welche Noten sich diese beziehen und finde heraus, wo in der Melodie sie auftauchen.

3. **Achte auf Muster**. Schaue dir die melodische Form an, während du den Rhythmus schlägst und achte auf Bewegungen in Schritten oder Sprüngen, sich wiederholende Noten und Sequenzen (eine kurze, sich wiederholende melodische Phrase, die oft schrittweise ansteigt oder abfällt).

4. **Artikulation und Dynamik**. Schaue dir die dynamischen Formen genau an und registriere, ob sie sich plötzlich oder allmählich ändern.

5. **Bleibe dran!**

Vortragsangaben, die in diesem Teil verwendet werden:

Allegretto	ziemlich lebhaft, aber langsamer als Allegro
Animato	belebt
Cantabile	gesangvoll
Con brio	mit Kraft
Con moto	mit Bewegung
Dolce	süß
Espressivo	ausdrucksvoll
Grazioso	anmutig
Legato	gebunden
Lento	langsam
Lilting	ein sanft schwingender Rhythmus
Maestoso	majestätisch
Moderato	gemäßigt
Vivace	lebhaft

Section 5 – Extending the range to top A
Section 5 – Extension de la tessiture jusqu'au *la* aigu
Teil 5 – Ausdehnung des Tonraums bis zum a²

In the keys of C, F and G major,
A, E and D minor.
Further use of dotted rhythms.

Tonalités majeures de *do, fa* et *sol*
et mineures de *la, mi* et *ré*. Autres
rythmes pointés.

Die Tonarten C-, F- und G-Dur,
A-, E- und D-Moll. Weitere Stücke
mit punktierten Noten.

The next three pieces are in E minor.
Watch out for the new D#.

Les trois pièces suivantes sont en
mi mineur. Attention au *ré*#.

Die folgenden drei Stücke sind in
E-Moll. Achte auf den neuen Ton Dis.

101.

102.

| The next three pieces are in D minor. Watch out for the new C♯. | Les trois pièces suivantes sont en *ré* mineur. Attention au *do*♯. | Die folgenden drei Stücke sind in D-Moll. Achte auf den neuen Ton Cis. |

103.

| This piece starts on the fourth beat of the bar. | Ces pièces débutent sur le 4ème temps de la mesure. | Dieses Stück beginnt auf den vierten Schlag des Takts. |

104.

| Look for the use of the melodic minor scale. | Observez l'utilisation de la gamme mineure mélodique. | Achte auf den Gebrauch der melodischen Molltonleiter. |

105.

The next two pieces are in A minor. Look for the use of the melodic minor scale. Count 1 2 3 before you begin.

Les deux pièces suivantes sont en *la* mineur. Observez l'utilisation de la gamme mineure mélodique. Comptez 1, 2, 3 avant de commencer.

Die folgenden zwei Stücke sind in A-Moll. Achte auf den Gebrauch der melodischen Molltonleiter. Zähle 1 2 3 bevor du beginnst.

106.

Count 1 2 3 1 2 before you begin.

Comptez 1, 2, 3, 1, 2, avant de commencer.

Zähle 1 2 3 1 2 vor, bevor du anfängst.

107.

Both parts in these duets may be played by the pupil and teacher or by two pupils.

Les deux parties de ce duo peuvent être jouées par l'élève et le professeur ou par deux élèves.

Beide Stimmen dieser Duette können von Schüler und Lehrer oder von zwei Schülern gespielt werden.

108.

109.

110.

111.

Lento e espressivo

This piece begins on the third beat in 3-time. Count 1 2 3 1 2 before you begin.

Cette pièce débute sur le 3e temps d'une mesure à 3 temps. Comptez 1, 2, 3, 1, 2, avant de commencer.

Dieses Stück beginnt auf dem dritten Schlag in einem 3/4-Takt. Zähle 1 2 3 1 2 vor, bevor du anfängst.

112.

Canon

This piece begins on the fourth beat in 4-time. Count 1 2 3 before you begin.

Cette pièce débute sur le 4e temps d'une mesure à 4 temps. Comptez 1, 2, 3, avant de commencer.

Dieses Stück beginnt auf dem vierten Schlag in einem 4/4-Takt. Zähle 1 2 3 vor, bevor du anfängst.

113.

Grazioso

114.

115.

116.

Try to sustain the long phrases fully.

Efforcez-vous de tenir les notes longues en entier.

Versuche die langen Phrasen konstant zu halten.

117.

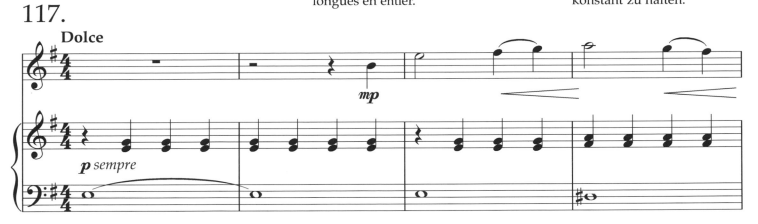

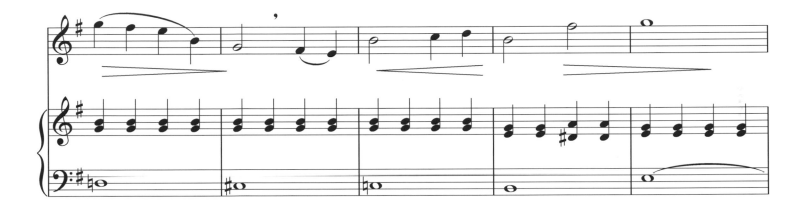

Section 6 – Introducing compound time
Section 6 – Introduction des mesures composées
Teil 6 – Einführung zusammengesetzter Taktarten

Six steps to success

1. **Look at the time signature**. Tap (clap, sing or play on one note) the rhythm, feeling the pulse throughout. Count at least one bar of the time signature in your head to set up the pulse before you tap or play each tune.

2. **Look between the treble clef and the time signature for any sharps or flats**. This is known as the key signature. Make sure you know which notes these apply to and notice where they occur in the melody. Sort out the fingerings before you begin.

3. **Look out for accidentals**. Check that you know the fingering before you arrive at the note.

4. **Look for patterns**. While tapping the rhythm, look at the melodic shape and notice movement by step, skips, repeated notes and sequences.

5. **Notice the articulation and dynamics**.

6. **Keep going!**

New performance directions:

Allegro	fast
Allegro ma non troppo	
	fast, but not too fast
Leggiero	lightly
Mesto	sadly
Poco	a little
Troppo	too much
Vivo	lively

Six étapes vers la réussite

1. **Observez l'indication de mesure**. Frappez (dans les mains, chantez ou jouez sur une seule note) le rythme tout en maintenant une pulsation intérieure constante. Comptez mentalement au moins une mesure pour installer la pulsation avant de frapper le rythme ou de jouer la pièce.

2. **Vérifiez les dièses ou les bémols placés entre la clef de *sol* et l'indication de mesure**. Ils constituent l'armure de la tonalité. Assurez-vous des notes altérées et repérez-les dans la mélodie. Pensez aux doigtés avant de commencer.

3. **Recherchez les altérations accidentelles**. Contrôlez votre doigté avant d'atteindre la note.

4. **Repérez les motifs**. Tout en frappant le rythme, observez les contours de la mélodie et relevez les mouvements par degrés, les sauts d'intervalles, les notes répétées et les séquences.

5. **Observez le phrasé et les nuances.**

6. **Ne vous arrêtez pas !**

Nouvelles indications d'exécution :

Allegro	rapide
Allegro ma non troppo	
	rapide mais pas trop
Leggiero	léger
Mesto	triste
Poco	peu
Troppo	trop
Vivo	vif

Sechs Schritte zum Erfolg

1. **Schaue dir die obere Zahl der Taktangabe an**. Diese zeigt die Anzahl der Schläge in einem Takt. Schlage (klatsche, singe oder spiele auf einer Note) den Rhythmus, wobei du immer das Metrum spürst. Zähle mindestens einen Takt lang die Taktangabe im Kopf, um das Metrum zu verinnerlichen, bevor du jede der Melodien klopfst oder spielst.

2. **Achte auf Kreuz- und B-Vorzeichen zwischen dem Notenschlüssel und der Taktangabe**. Versichere dich, dass du weißt, auf welche Noten sich diese beziehen und finde heraus, wo in der Melodie sie auftauchen.

3. **Suche nach Notenvorzeichen**. Stelle sicher, dass du die Greifweise kennst, bevor du diese Note erreichst.

4. **Achte auf Muster**. Schaue dir die melodische Form an, während du den Rhythmus schlägst und achte auf Bewegungen in Schritten oder Sprüngen, sich wiederholende Noten und Sequenzen.

5. **Beachte Artikulation und Dynamik.**

6. **Bleibe dran!**

Neue Vortragsangaben:

Allegro	schnell
Allegro ma non troppo	
	schnell, aber nicht zu schnell
Leggioro	leicht
Mesto	traurig
Poco	ein wenig
Troppo	zu viel
Vivo	lebhaft

Key steps to understanding compound rhythms

1. 6/8, 9/8 and 12/8 are known as compound time signatures. Each beat is divided into three equal parts (say the word 'elephant' to a beat), unlike simple time signatures (2/4, 3/4 and 4/4), which divide into two equal parts (say the word 'tiger' to a beat).

2. 6/8 is the most common of these time signatures and means six equal quavers (eighth notes) in a bar. In 6/8 there are two groups of three quavers (eighth notes), so each bar has two beats and will be counted in two.

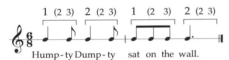

3. The opening two bars of 'Humpty Dumpty' contain the three most common rhythms found in compound time signatures.

4. In all compound time signatures

♩. = two beats

♪. = one beat

♩ = two thirds of a beat

♪ = one third of a beat

5.
6/8 is two beats in a bar
(two groups of three quavers)

9/8 is three beats in a bar
(three groups of three quavers)

12/8 is four beats in a bar
(four groups of three quavers)

Etapes essentielles à la compréhension des mesures composées

1. 6/8, 9/8 et 12/8 constituent les indications de mesures composées. Chaque temps y est divisé en trois parties égales (prononcez le mot « éléphant » sur chaque temps) à la différence des mesures simples (2/4, 3/4, et 4/4) dont les temps se divisent en deux parties égales (prononcez les mot « canard » sur chaque temps).

2. 6/8 est l'indication de mesure composée la plus fréquente et signifie que chaque mesure contient six croches égales. Chaque mesure à 6/8 contient deux groupes de trois croches. C'est donc une mesure à deux temps.

3. Les deux premières mesures de *Humpty Dumpty* présentent les trois rythmes les plus fréquemment rencontrés dans les mesures composées.

4. Dans toutes les mesures composées

♩. = deux temps

♪. = un temps

♩ = deux tiers de temps

♪ = un tiers de temps

5.
6/8 indique deux temps par mesure
(deux groupes de trois croches)

9/8 indique trois temps par mesure
(trois groupes de trois croches)

12/8 indique quatre temps par mesure
(quatre groupes de trois croches)

Die entscheidenden Schritte, um zusammengesetzte Rhythmen zu verstehen

1. 6/8, 9/8 und 12/8 sind als zusammengesetzte Taktarten bekannt. Jeder Schlag ist in drei gleichlange Teile aufgeteilt (sage das Wort ‚Murmeltier' auf einen Schlag) im Gegensatz zu einfachen Taktarten (2/4, 3/4 und 4/4), die in zwei gleichlange Teile aufgeteilt sind (sage das Wort ‚Tiger' auf einen Schlag).

2. Von diesen Taktarten kommt der 6/8-Takt am häufigsten vor. Er besteht aus sechs gleichlangen Achteln in einem Takt. Im 6/8-Takt gibt es zwei Gruppen mit je drei Achtelnoten. Jeder Takt hat also zwei Schläge und wird auf zwei gezählt.

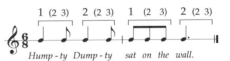

3. Die Eröffnungstakte des Kinderliedes *Humpty Dumpty* beinhalten die drei häufigsten Rhythmen, die man in zusammengesetzten Taktarten finden kann.

4. In allen zusammengesetzten Taktarten sind

♩. = zwei Schläge

♪. = ein Schlag

♩ = 2/3 eines Schlages

♪ = 1/3 eines Schlages

5.
6/8 hat zwei Schläge in einem Takt
(zwei Gruppen mit drei Achteln)

9/8 hat drei Schläge in einem Takt
(drei Gruppen mit drei Achteln)

12/8 hat vier Schläge in einem Takt
(vier Gruppen mit drei Achteln)

Section 6 – Introducing compound time
Section 6 – Introduction des mesures composées
Teil 6 – Einführung zusammengesetzter Taktarten

Time signatures of **3***, **6** and **9** Exploring new keys.	Mesures à **3**, **6** et **9** Nouvelles tonalités.	Die Taktangaben **3**, **6** und **9** und neue Tonarten.

* Although strictly simple time, 3/8 often takes on the characteristic of a compound time signature.
  It was therefore decided to include 3/8 pieces in this section.

This piece begins on the third beat of the bar in 3-time.
Count 1 2 3 1 2 before you begin.

Cette pièce débute sur le 3e temps d'une mesure à 3 temps.
Comptez 1, 2, 3, 1, 2, avant de commencer.

Dieses Stück beginnt auf dem dritten Schlag in einem 3/4-Takt.
Zähle 1 2 3 1 2 vor, bevor du anfängst.

122.

Introducing semiquavers (♪)

Introduction des doubles croches (♪)

Einführung von Sechzehnteln (♪)

123.

This piece begins on the third beat of the bar in 3-time.
Count 1 2 3 1 2 before you begin.

Cette pièce débute sur le 3e temps d'une mesure à 3 temps.
Comptez 1, 2, 3, 1, 2, avant de commencer.

Dieses Stück beginnt auf dem dritten Schlag in einem 3/4-Takt.
Zähle 1 2 3 1 2 vor, bevor du anfängst.

124.

New time: $\frac{6}{8}$

Nouvelle mesure à $\frac{6}{8}$

Neue Taktart: $\frac{6}{8}$

125.

126.

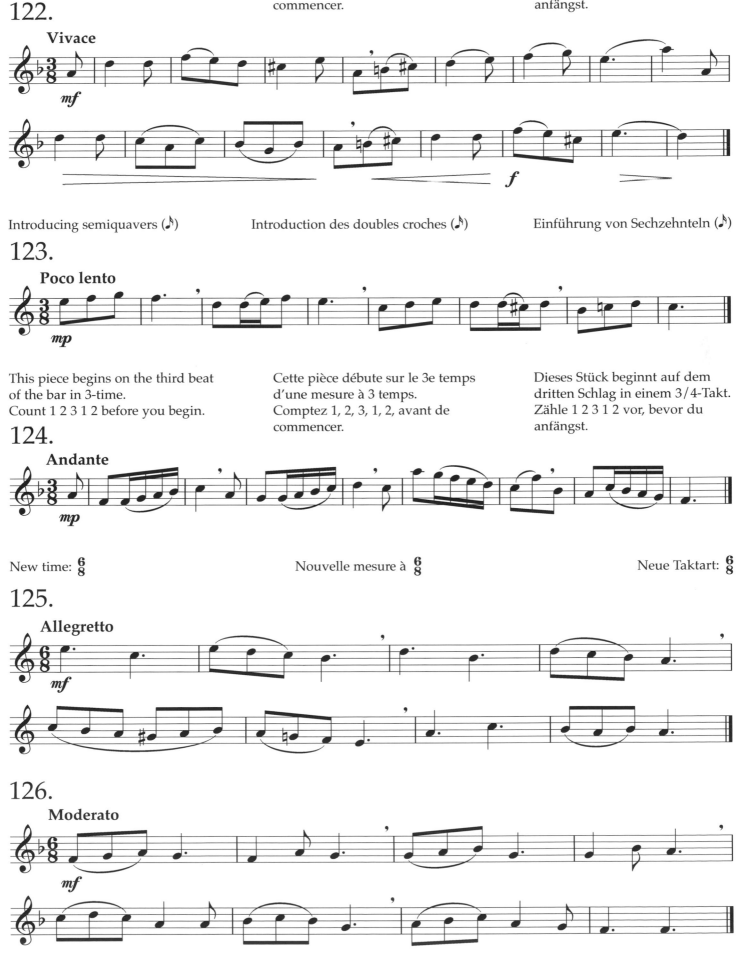

48

The next two pieces are in G minor. Look out for the new E♭.

This piece begins on the fifth quaver in **6/8** time.

Count 1 (2 3) 2 before you begin.

Les deux pièces suivantes sont en *sol* mineur. Attention au *mi*♭.

Cette pièce débute sur la 5ème croche d'une mesure à **6/8**.

Comptez 1 (2, 3), 2 avant de commencer.

Die folgenden zwei Stücke sind in G-Moll. Achte auf den neuen Ton Es.

Dieses Stück beginnt auf der fünften Achtel im **6/8**-Takt.

Zähle 1 (2 3) 2 bevor Du beginnst.

127.

Andante

This piece begins on the last quaver of the bar. Remember to count before you begin.

Cette pièce débute sur la dernière croche de la mesure. N'oubliez pas de compter avant de commencer.

Dieses Stück beginnt auf der lezten Achtel des Takts. Denke daran zu zählen bevor du beginnst.

128.

Mesto
(Modal)

Remember to count before you begin.

N'oubliez pas de compter avant de commencer.

Denke daran zu zählen bevor du beginnst.

129.

Grazioso

130.

Vivo

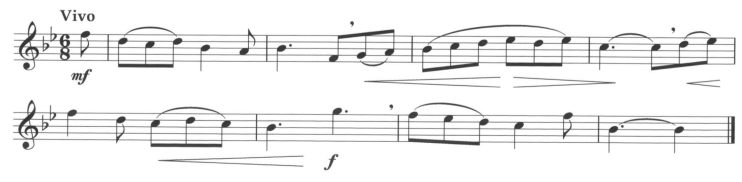

This is the new key of D major. Look out for the new C♯ in the key signature.

Nouvelle tonalité de *ré* majeur. Attention au *do*♯ à l'armure de la clef.

Die neue Tonart D-Dur. Achte auf den neuen Ton Cis.

131.

This is in the new key of C minor. Your new note is A♭.

Nouvelle tonalité de *do* mineur. Nouvelle note *la*♭.

Die neue Tonart C-Moll. Dein neuer Ton ist As.

132.

133.

New time: **9/8**
Count 1 (2 3) 2 (2 3) 3 (2 3).

Nouvelle mesure à **9/8**
Comptez 1 (2, 3), 2 (2, 3), 3 (2, 3).

Neue Taktart: **9/8**
Zähle 1 (2 3) 2 (2 3) 3 (2 3) bevor du beginnst.

134.

135.

136.

137.

138.

139.

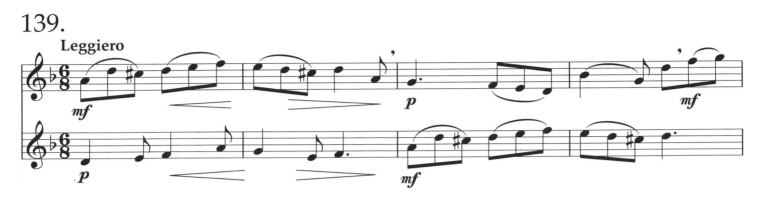

140.

141.

142.

Allegro

143.

Allegretto

144.

Vivace

145.

146.

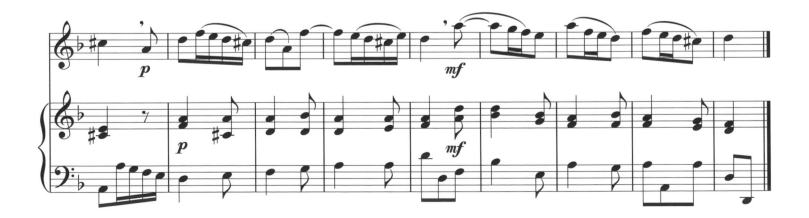

147.

Section 7 – Increasing range: low E♭/D♯ to high B♭/B♮
Section 7 – Extension de la tessiture : de *mi♭* grave/*ré♯* grave à *si♭* aigu/*si♮* aigu
Teil 7 – Zunehmender Tonraum: von es^1/dis^1 bis zum b^2/h^2

Six steps to success

1. **Look at the time signature.** Tap (clap, sing or play on one note) the rhythm, feeling the pulse throughout. Count at least one bar of the time signature in your head to set up the pulse before you tap or play each tune.

2. **Look between the treble clef and the time signature for any sharps or flats.** This is known as the key signature. Make sure you know which notes these apply to and notice where they occur in the melody. Sort out the fingerings before you begin.

3. **Look out for accidentals.** Check that you know the fingering before you arrive at the note.

4. **Look for patterns.** While tapping the rhythm, look at the melodic shape and notice movement by step, skips, repeated notes and sequences.

5. **Notice the articulation and dynamics.**

6. **Keep going!**

New performance directions:
Capriccioso	light-heartedly
Diminuendo (*dim.*)	becoming gradually softer
Largamente	broadly
Pesante	heavily
Più mosso	more movement/faster
Ritmico	rhythmically
Scherzando	playfully
Sostenuto	sustained
Veloce	swift/quick

Six étapes vers la réussite

1. **Observez l'indication de mesure.** Frappez (dans les mains, chantez ou jouez sur une seule note) le rythme tout en maintenant une pulsation intérieure constante. Comptez mentalement au moins une mesure pour installer la pulsation avant de frapper le rythme ou de jouer la pièce.

2. **Vérifiez les dièses ou les bémols placés entre la clef de *sol* et l'indication de mesure.** Ils constituent l'armure de la tonalité. Assurez-vous des notes altérées et repérez-les dans la mélodie. Pensez aux doigtés avant de commencer.

3. **Recherchez les altérations accidentelles.** Contrôlez votre doigté avant d'atteindre la note.

4. **Repérez les motifs.** Tout en frappant le rythme, observez les contours de la mélodie et relevez les mouvements par degrés, les sauts d'intervalles, les notes répétées et les séquences.

5. **Observez le phrasé et les nuances.**

6. **Ne vous arrêtez pas !**

Nouvelles indications d'exécution :
Capriccioso	capricieux
Diminuendo (*dim.*)	en diminuant
Largamente	largement
Pesante	pesamment
Più mosso	plus vite
Ritmico	rythmé
Scherzando	en badinant
Sostenuto	soutenu
Veloce	rapide/vite

Sechs Schritte zum Erfolg

1. **Schaue dir die obere Zahl der Taktangabe an.** Diese zeigt die Anzahl der Schläge in einem Takt. Schlage (klatsche, singe oder spiele auf einer Note) den Rhythmus, wobei du immer das Metrum spürst. Zähle mindestens einen Takt lang die Taktangabe im Kopf, um das Metrum zu verinnerlichen, bevor du jede der Melodien klopfst oder spielst.

2. **Achte auf Kreuz- und B-Vorzeichen zwischen dem Notenschlüssel und der Taktangabe.** Versichere dich, dass du weißt, auf welche Noten sich diese beziehen und finde heraus, wo in der Melodie sie auftauchen.

3. **Suche nach Notenvorzeichen.** Stelle sicher, dass du die Greifweise kennst, bevor du diese Note erreichst.

4. **Achte auf Muster.** Schaue dir die melodische Form an, während du den Rhythmus schlägst und achte auf Bewegungen in Schritten oder Sprüngen, sich wiederholende Noten und Sequenzen.

5. **Beachte Artikulation und Dynamik.**

6. **Bleibe dran!**

Neue Vortragszeichen:
Capriccioso	unbeschwert
Diminuendo (*dim.*)	allmählich weicher werden
Largamente	breit
Pesante	schwer
Più mosso	Bewegung/schneller
Ritmico	rhythmisch
Scherzando	spielerisch
Sostenuto	zurückhaltend
Veloce	geschwind/schnell

Section 7 – Increasing range: low E♭/D♯ to high B♭/B♮

Section 7 – Extension de la tessiture : de *mi♭* grave/*ré♯* grave à *si♭* aigu/*si♮* aigu

Teil 7 – Zunehmender Tonraum: von es¹/dis¹ bis zum b²/h²

153.

Ritmico capriccioso

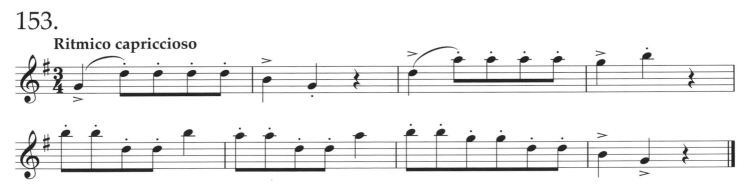

154.

Lento e espressivo

155.

Cantabile e legato

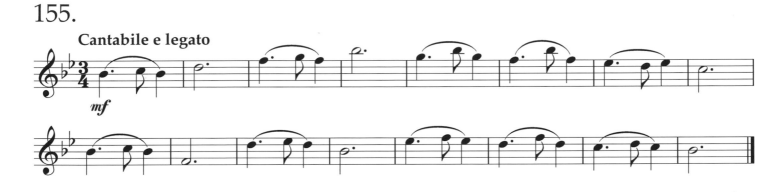

156.

Pesante

157.

Vivace

158.

159.

160.

161.

162.

163.

164.

165.

166.

60

167.

168.

169.

170.

171.

172.

173.

174.

175.

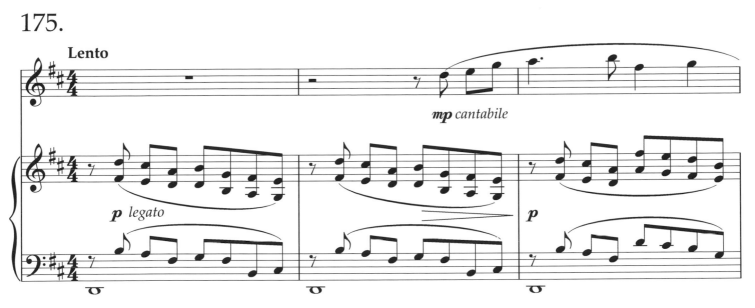

176.

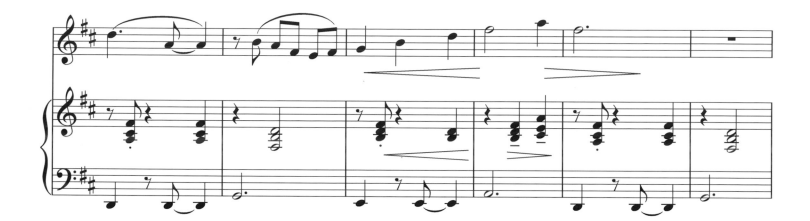

Section 8 – Semiquavers in simple and compound times
Section 8 – Doubles croches dans les mesures simples et les mesures composées
Teil 8 – Sechzehntelnoten in einfachen und zusammengesetzten Taktarten

Six steps to success

1. **Look at the time signature**. Tap (clap, sing or play on one note) the rhythm, feeling the pulse throughout. Count at least one bar of the time signature in your head to set up the pulse before you tap or play each tune.

2. **Look between the treble clef and the time signature for any sharps or flats**. This is known as the key signature. Make sure you know which notes these apply to and notice where they occur in the melody. Sort out the fingerings before you begin.

3. **Look out for accidentals**. Check that you know the fingering before you arrive at the note.

4. **Look for patterns**. While tapping the rhythm, look at the melodic shape and notice movement by step, skip, repeated notes and sequences.

5. **Notice the articulation and dynamics**.

6. **Keep going!**

Before you start this section, it might help to remind yourself of the performance directions you have learned.

Six étapes vers la réussite

1. **Observez l'indication de mesure**. Frappez (dans les mains, chantez ou jouez sur une seule note) le rythme tout en maintenant une pulsation intérieure constante. Comptez mentalement au moins une mesure pour installer la pulsation avant de frapper le rythme ou de jouer la pièce.

2. **Vérifiez les dièses ou les bémols placés entre la clef de *sol* et l'indication de mesure**. Ils constituent l'armure de la tonalité. Assurez-vous des notes altérées et repérez-les dans la mélodie. Pensez aux doigtés avant de commencer.

3. **Recherchez les altérations accidentelles**. Contrôlez votre doigté avant d'atteindre la note.

4. **Repérez les motifs**. Tout en frappant le rythme, observez les contours de la mélodie et relevez les mouvements par degrés, les sauts d'intervalles, les notes répétées et les séquences.

5. **Observez le phrasé et les nuances**.

6. **Ne vous arrêtez pas !**

Avant de vous attaquez à cette section, il vous sera sans doute utile de vous rappeler les indications d'exécution que vous avez apprises.

Sechs Schritte zum Erfolg

1. **Schaue dir die obere Zahl der Taktangabe an**. Diese zeigt die Anzahl der Schläge in einem Takt. Schlage (klatsche, singe oder spiele auf einer Note) den Rhythmus, wobei du immer das Metrum spürst. Zähle mindestens einen Takt lang die Taktangabe im Kopf, um das Metrum zu verinnerlichen, bevor du jede der Melodien klopfst oder spielst.

2. **Achte auf Kreuz- und B-Vorzeichen zwischen dem Notenschlüssel und der Taktangabe**. Versichere dich, dass du weißt, auf welche Noten sich diese beziehen und finde heraus, wo in der Melodie sie auftauchen.

3. **Suche nach Notenvorzeichen**. Stelle sicher, dass du die Greifweise kennst, bevor du diese Note erreichst.

4. **Achte auf Muster**. Schaue dir die melodische Form an, während du den Rhythmus schlägst und achte auf Bewegungen in Schritten oder Sprüngen, sich wiederholende Noten und Sequenzen.

5. **Beachte Artikulation und Dynamik**.

6. **Bleibe dran!**

Bevor du mit diesem Teil beginnst, könnte es eventuell hilfreich sein, dir noch einmal die Vortragszeichen in Erinnerung zu rufen, die du bereits gelernt hast.

Section 8 – Semiquavers in simple and compound times
Section 8 – Doubles croches dans les mesures simples et les mesures composées
Teil 8 – Sechzehntelnoten in einfachen und zusammengesetzten Taktarten

177.

178.

179.

180.

181.

182.

183.

184.

185.

186.

187.

188.

Con moto

189.

Mesto

190.

Poco lento

191.

192.

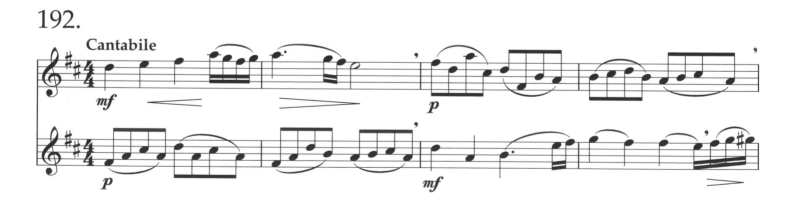

193.

194.

195.

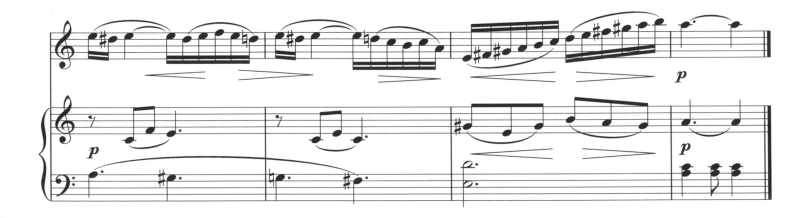

196.

Glossary
Glossaire
Glossar

Note performance directions together with their translations used throughout the book so that you have a complete list. Writing them down will help you to remember them.

Inscrivez ici les indications d'exécution utilisées dans ce volume et leur traduction pour en établir une liste complète. Le fait de les noter vous aidera à les retenir.

Schreibe hier alle Vortragszeichen, die im Buch verwendet werden, zusammen mit ihrer Übersetzung auf, so dass du eine vollständige Liste hast. Das Aufschreiben wird dir dabei helfen, sie dir einzuprägen.

Adagio	Slowly	Lent	Langsam
